M000309956

Any collaboration with local people is a good thing – but the best collaboration is spiritual. It is where we begin to pray together about the community, and the emerging ministry. In such a spiritual collaboration, amazing things begin to happen.

Paul Nixon

CULTURAL COMPETENCY

*Partnering with Your Neighbors
in Your Ministry Expedition*

PAUL NIXON

the greatest
EXPEDITION

CULTURAL COMPETENCY
Partnering with Your Neighbors in Your Ministry Expedition

©2021 Paul Nixon

books@marketsquarebooks.com
P.O. Box 23664   Knoxville, Tennessee 37933
ISBN: 978-1-950899-20-3
Library of Congress: 2021931131

Printed and Bound in the United States of America
Cover Illustration & Book Design ©2021 Market Square Publishing, LLC
Publisher: Kevin Slimp
Editors: Kristin Lighter and Kay Kotan
Post-Process Editor: Ken Rochelle

All rights reserved. No part of this book may be reproduced in any
manner without written permission except in the case of brief quotations
included in critical articles and reviews. For information, please contact
Market Square Publishing, LLC.

This resource was commissioned as
one of many interconnected steps in the
journey of *The Greatest Expedition.*

the greatest
EXPEDITION

GreatestExpedition.com

Table of Contents

Foreword, by Kay Kotan 1

Ever Been to Mars? 3

Baselines 13

   The Christian Good News transcends culture. 17

   Your Church belongs to God, not to you. 21

   The Good Ole' Days are in front of us, not behind us 24

   Authenticity is essential – don't try to be something
   or somebody that you are not 28

   No church can serve everybody – so each church
   had better get focused on particular somebodies. 32

   Friendship first, then ministry development 36

   Cultural competency requires spiritual readiness 41

   Social privilege often gets in our way 46

   Community partnerships are priceless 50

   Good listening may lead to un-learning, which leads
   to even better listening. 52

   A lot of what we try will go about as well as a
   Wile E. Coyote scheme 57

   God is alive and at work in every neighborhood. Our
   challenge is to show up to what God is doing 59

   Regardless of strategy, spiritual collaboration
   with new people is essential 62

Strategies and Your Church's Ministry Expedition 67

Cultural Competency Began as a Work of the Holy Spirit . . . 91

FOREWORD

By Kay Kotan

This resource was commissioned as one of many interconnected steps in the journey of *The Greatest Expedition*. While each step is important individually, we Intentionally built the multi-step Essentials Pack and the Expansion Pack to provide a richer and fuller experience with the greatest potential for transformation and introducing more people to a relationship with Jesus Christ. For more information visit GreatestExpedition.org.

However, we also recognize you may be exploring this resource apart from *The Greatest Expedition*. You might find yourself on a personal journey, a small group journey, or perhaps a church leadership team journey. We are so glad you are on this journey!

As you take each step in your expedition, your Expedition Team will discover whether the ministry tools you will be exploring will be utilized only for the Expedition Team or if this expedition will be a congregational journey. Our hope and prayer is *The Greatest Expedition* is indeed a congregational journey, but if it proves to be a solo journey for just the Expedition Team, God will still do amazing things through your intentional exploration, discernment, and faithful next steps.

Regardless of how you came to discover *The Greatest Expedition,* it will pave the way to a new God-inspired expedition. Be brave and courageous on your journey through *The Greatest Expedition!*

Kay L Kotan, PCC
Director, *The Greatest Expedition*

Ever Been to Mars?

Have you ever found yourself on a distant planet, far from the Earth you've known? Okay, not literally – but can you recall a time when you looked around and realized you were not in Kansas anymore? Or Arizona? Or in your family-of-origin neighborhood where most people saw the world as you see it? Or in a place where you did not know how to start a simple conversation?

Lots of folks move or migrate from one place to another. Sometimes across oceans, other times from rural to urban within their country (or vice versa). And yet, if you grew up in small town Iowa and then found yourself working in downtown Chicago, you may not have to look hard to find other displaced Iowans and people who share your life experience and values. And if you moved from Houston out to a small community 70 miles north where new housing was under development, you might fall in to the slower pace of life relatively easily, perhaps rediscovering some of your grandparents' culture.

On the other hand, if you moved from the Los Angeles area to the rural South (or vice versa), you know something about travel to Mars.

Or consider this story: I have a friend whose parents were Chinese peasants. They moved from rural China to New York City fifty years ago. And, today they still neither speak nor read any English. They ran a little restaurant in Queens cooking recipes from back home, and found plenty of customers. But whenever they wander more than a few blocks from home in any direction, they are on Mars. Their son adjusted well – got an Ivy League degree and became one of the Martians. That, too, must feel a little weird.

A few years ago, on the way to visit my mother-in-law in Taiwan, we spent a few days in Beijing. As we came out of the Forbidden City (a setting where most western tourists would feel comfortable), we discovered a bus that was about to depart for the Great Wall. Round trip bus transportation, lunch and tickets to the Great Wall – for twenty American dollars. A six-hour adventure. We said, "Why not? It's a great deal." As we stepped onto the bus, it was clear that only then did we fully enter China. As the only White person aboard, I could feel all eyes focusing on me as we moved up the aisle in search of empty seats. At one point the tour guide pointed my way and told people to mind their manners and not spit because "we had a very special guest on board." (White privilege even here!) This only increased the sense of disconnection that I felt with the other people around me.

Given the budget the tour company had to work with, the food at lunch was not very good – simple and starchy slop, even by local standards. The meal was served family style in a gigantic dining hall. Most of the people at our table were college age. They ate with gusto. They were kind and asked me (in Mandarin) if I would like seconds before they inhaled the last of it. Most of the table conversation was in dialect that even my Mandarin-speaking spouse could not understand. If you asked me about a time I felt like I was on Mars, this day trip to the Great Wall of China is the first thing that would come to my mind.

And now, I am asking you:

When and where did you ever feel like you were on Mars, out of your element?

Sometimes, one does not have to move at all to get this feeling. Every zip code in America is a changing neighborhood these days, in terms of generational tastes if not in other ways.

People might live in the same house for several decades and watch things change over time. The change can go in almost any direction. Anglo neighborhoods became Latin or Vietnamese. Black neighborhoods become primarily Anglo. And every neighborhood has young adult children who just don't relate to church (or Kiwanis Club, Eastern Star, etc.) the way their parents did.

A local factory closes and within five years, the number of middle class families left in the community is cut in half. They are replaced by various kinds of new folks, almost all financially struggling.

Small town neighborhoods shrink in population and lose their high school, which means long school bus rides into the county seat. Or all those Houstonians move in to the new subdivision that means a bigger, newer school right in the community – but with a suburban vibe that is so...very...Martian.

In my current Washington DC neighborhood, settled by people of mostly English origins, the neighborhood has shifted every two or three decades for 200 years. Mary Surratt's boarding house down the street, where confederate sympathizers plotted to assassinate Lincoln, is now a Sushi bar – that should tell you something.

And churches. They are not as portable as families. Imagine a church in, say, the Harlem section of New York City, where most of the participants grew up within walking distance of the church house, decades ago. Now half of them are retired up in Westchester County – and on Sundays, they commute back to a place that holds powerful meaning and memory for them personally. But they have almost no interaction with Harlem people anymore, nor do they design their ministry for Harlem people anymore.

They may not even buy the Sunday donuts for fellowship time in Harlem. They commute in and commute out. And the local people around that church house: if they don't play close attention between 9 am and 1 pm on Sunday, they might never see signs of human life in or around the building.

Meanwhile, the neighborhood around the church is as vibrant as ever: filled with a new generation of homeowners, an ever-shifting mix of people, new political sensibilities, a new language or two. There are thousands upon thousands of such churches in North America, in every sort of community. Once the building hits its fiftieth birthday, the chances are good that Martian weather conditions are setting in around it. When the church members head out the church doors toward their cars, they could as well be darting across the surface of Mars. They haven't a clue how to begin a meaningful ministry conversation with the people who live across the street.

In all fairness, some churches were never really geographically rooted. Many churches are regional magnet locations for people seeking a certain kind of experience, people scattered across a wide territory. But then, the population that sought that experience gets older, and their kids grow up and choose different kinds of churches or weekend experiences. The end result is the same: a church that finds itself increasingly isolated from the world around it.

Do you feel that your church is as well connected to its mission zone, as it would have been 25 years ago? Why or why not?

Most people reading this book will answer that their church's engagement with the community around it is more challenged today than 25 years ago. That is just where we find ourselves in the 2020s. A few of you will joyfully celebrate just the opposite. In the latter case, where a church remains deeply in sync with the culture outside its walls, it is likely that major changes have occurred within that church's life. Worship has probably changed enormously – as has almost every other ministry in the church's life. The church empowered a new generation of leaders and followed their lead.

In the pages ahead we explore how a church can regain a sense of cultural competency for ministering to the world around it. There are different strategies that impact how we do this – no single strategy is right for every church. But there are also baseline principles that are universally applicable. We will look first at a few baselines of culturally competent ministry, and then consider the varied strategies churches employ to get back in the game, in terms of effective ministry with their neighbors.

Baselines

A baseline is a norm from which we all can work. Many cities have a Baseline Avenue or Road, which dates back to the earliest days of that city when surveyors would draw a line, called the *base line,* that helped create a starting point for the development of a street grid. It often was drawn in reference to true north, south, east and west. The term may also refer to a boundary for a field of play in baseball, basketball or tennis. The Gospel of Jesus provides serious baseline for us in all that we do. Any principle related to the work of ministering across cultures that is truly baseline would have to be always true. With that in mind, I offer the following baselines.

With each baseline, I have asked, and asked again, "Is this always true?" In inter-cultural work, we may discover that something we ranked up there as dependable as Gospel is in fact a reflection of our own cultural or political perspective – and not accepted among most Christian believers. It may be an important idea for us – but it will not hold water for everyone who follows Christ, especially if they were not raised in our part of the world, within our denomination or with our access (or lack of access) to money. So baselines are tricky. There is nothing wrong with embracing an idea that we feel is important, even when we know that there are those within the church who see it differently. But we might want to be careful about calling that baseline. This is especially true when the church we are praying for contains considerable diversity of people.

One aspect of cultural competency is keeping track of what rises to the level of baseline and what is a simply a strong conviction for us personally or for our family. An example of the latter would be: A church or a family should always stay out of debt. No financial advisor could say this in absolute terms, but we have all known amazing people and churches that just refused to borrow money. They saved until they could pay cash – or otherwise did without. Another example would be my Mom's conviction that life is just better without any alcoholic beverages, all the way to the finish line.

> **Can you think of another example of a conviction might seem almost like a baseline for you, but where you can see that some really great people of faith might not buy it?**

> You are saying: "This is important to me, but I am going to stop short of saying for sure that it is God's will for every human being." And you are not going to let disagreement on this become an issue in terms of a new ministry.

With each baseline that is listed below, I have been unable to think of exceptions. So they stayed on my list. If you can think of an exception to one, then perhaps I have misjudged. I do that sometimes. In that case, you should enjoy a robust conversation with your church's ministry team as you evaluate that idea – and improve it.

- The Christian Good News transcends culture.
- Your church belongs to God, not to you.
- The Good Ole Days are in front of us, not behind us.
- Authenticity is essential – don't try to be something (or somebody) that you are not.
- No church can serve everybody – so each church had better get focused on particular somebodies.
- Friendship first, then ministry development.
- Cultural competency requires spiritual readiness.
- Social privilege often gets in our way.
- Community partnerships are priceless.
- Good listening may lead to un-learning, which leads to even better listening.
- A lot of what we try will go about as well as a Wile E. Coyote scheme.
- God is alive and at work in every neighborhood – our challenge is to show up to what God is doing.
- Regardless of strategy, spiritual collaboration with new people is essential.

1. The Christian Good News transcends culture

Christianity originated with a group of first century Middle Eastern Jews living under a cruel colonial occupation by an external power. It has spread around the world into a variety of cultures and political systems. The process of hopping boundaries is rooted in what occurred on the Day of Pentecost. Every time we seek to adapt it from one context to the next, significant interpretation and adjustments are made.

Certainly we make mistakes in this kind of work. However, we can take comfort that the process of hopping human boundaries began on the Day of Pentecost, and was fundamentally the work of the Holy Spirit. It was not as if the Apostles and friends were huddled in the Upper Room reading position papers to one another on how to do contextual evangelism.

Every time, Christianity takes root in a new cultural context, there is transference of key faith content that forms the core. Alongside this, there are elements of practice that either fall by the wayside or are significantly altered, possibly emphasized anew. These shifts sometimes came with considerable controversy – and even organizational schism.

But the shifts are only possible because of a continuity of common core in our faith, tying us together across the centuries. In the Book of Acts, as the Apostles began to share the faith across the Roman Empire, we see a common core of material in the sermons they preached. That core (sometimes called the *kerygma*) typically included:

- The significance of the Christ event (life, death and resurrection of Jesus) as the central event of history, after creation. Everything is transformed and redeemed because of this event.

- Connecting the dots between the Christ event and the earlier cultural history and faith traditions of the listeners.

- The personal story of how the speaker's life was personally impacted because of her/his encounter with Christ.

Within most of our denominational traditions there is additional common core – which often can be adapted to almost any cultural context on earth, especially if the Holy Spirit is driving things.

Examples of shifts or adaptations:

- As widespread literacy spread across Christian populations, and people were able to directly study the Bible, the understanding of clergy as priests went into decline in many places, and the idea of 'priesthood of every believer' rose in emphasis.

- As women's education and leadership in society began to catch up to that of men, women's roles also shifted in the church.

- Most societies today have no tradition of blood sacrifice. Neither do most people expect that their mistakes and transgressions in relationships can be erased by punishment. When broken relationships are restored, it usually has little to do with punishment. Rather, people come to regret their actions, and seek forgiveness from those they have harmed. (Jesus' parable of the prodigal son thus becomes one of the most significant passages for a lot of modern people, because it resonates so powerfully with our experience of relationship. Paul's writings in his letter Romans on the Law are now a bit of a snoozer for many.) So, we may hear fewer songs these days in worship singing about the blood of Jesus, and more about the transforming love of Jesus. The cross may shift from representing a punishment taken on our behalf to appease God's honor (which made a lot of sense to Europeans in medieval times) to representing the tenacity of God's commitment to love us in human flesh, even to the point of experiencing the horrors of the cross.

These are each examples of how the Gospel (Christian Good News) is able to retain its power in our lives, even as we undergo cultural shifts.

During the 1990s, a major focus of my own ministry was to take historic Christianity, in its Methodist expression, and adapt that to the lives and sensibilities of people in a Florida beach community. This was possible only after a few years immersed in that culture, getting a sense of how people thought, the things that gave them joy and the challenges that they confronted in life.

Our church planted a series of new worship communities, each designed around the life situation of a rather niche population. Core content did not change, but the way we gathered for worship changed radically from one service to the next. The kind of music, the flow and pace of the gathering, the use of humor, the style of preaching/teaching, informality – we made changes on every front, resulting in effective connection with hundreds of new people. For many of these people, organized religion had not made much sense to them. For others, it had deeply disappointed them. Most of this disconnect was cultural – and was not primarily an argument with the core of Christian faith.

Because we sought to create a space where our neighbors could discover the transforming love of God, the following occurred:

- **New kinds of people began to make our church their spiritual home.**

- **People who had been spiritually amorphous (and all over the place in their ideas) began to take on a more Christ-defined shape in their lives.**

- **Some people who had been in our church a while were annoyed – by changes in worship, by our not starting right on time (when our crowd liked to come in ten minutes late), and by the music which was often criticized as too (fill in the blank). Always too much this or that.**

Baseline: God is not limited to our culture. This leads right in to the next base line.

2. Your church belongs to God, not to you.

At first glance, this may seem like a no-brainer. Most of us understand at an intellectual level that the church belongs to God and we are just stewards of the treasure. And yet, stewarding the church can quickly become *guard-dogging* it, if we are not careful. It is human nature – on every continent – that some folks will begin to defend their church from everybody and everything outside it.

I have seen a church in the South that stopped their annual Vacation Bible School rather than to allow it to receive children of different races. I have seen a church in the Northeast cover much of the furniture in the church building in plastic wrap for fear that someone (especially kids) might scratch something or get it dirty. I have seen many places where a certain painting or wall-hanging could not be moved from a certain spot because it was given by someone's mother or because it was a portrait of a beloved pastor from long ago or because it had always hung in that spot. Since the days of Noah. In that spot.

Inevitably, the mission of the church to reach new people means renovating church lobbies to make them welcoming. And the wall art is not the core we seek to preserve. Nor is it really ever appropriate to protect a church building from the population around it. This is not stewarding the treasure of the church – it is guard dogging.

If the church belongs to God, then God's purposes and mission over-ride our own preferences and traditions. A church building exists as a tool to reach and serve new people, not to memorialize past people.

My dad was a pastor, and so we moved every few years from one church to the next. There are three churches on earth that became places of significant spiritual formation for me. They are still important places to me – even after several decades. Over the years, I have gone back occasionally to each of the three. In each case, these are still vital and life-giving places – which is notable. But most of the people I knew in each place have either departed or they have aged so that I would be unable to identify them in a police line up.

However, there is one big reason why these are still such vibrant churches. They have each changed over the years. None of the three resisted the changes that were necessary in order to follow the Holy Spirit into a new millennium. Across decades, they really practiced what they had preached.

I took my mom back to visit one of these churches a few years back. The changes were so jarring that it took all of Sunday lunch for us to debrief our trauma. Ha! It had been such a formal, almost regal place of worship for many decades. My mom used to say of that town, that she liked it because it never seemed to change. Now the pastor led worship in cowboy boots and an un-tucked shirt, standing floor level with the congregation. But we concluded that the church was probably more true to the culture of small town central Texas today than it had been fifty years ago. And while some aspects of worship did not feel comfortable for us – I expect, based on the people gathered in the room that day, that they have a very good future in that community. I suspect that God is pleased with the choices they have made – even if it would drive crazy the people who used to run things there.

Baseline: Church is, first of all, God's thing.

3. The Good Ole' Days are in front of us, not behind us.

Most churches today have fewer people than they had a decade ago. There are wonderful exceptions to that statement, but they are exceptions. Having worked with hundreds of churches, I have never observed God's presence as limited only to churches that have grown in recent years. In fact, I find amazing ministry, creativity, compassion, prophecy, servant-hood and more in all sorts of churches, including churches in decline. Generations pass, neighborhoods shift, society secularizes – but my goodness, there are some beautiful, tenacious faith communities sprinkled across the earth. I love it when churches move from decline to a new season of thriving – those are always special experiences. But how often we discover that the new thriving normal entails a much smaller congregation than gathered "back in the day."

It is easy to glorify yesterday. It is easy to forget the troubles of another era and remember selectively. Sometimes the spiritual victories of today do not correlate with enormous crowds in the sanctuary.

As we move deeper into the 2020s, with the emerging hybrid ministry model of both on-site and online gathering, the average on-site crowd size for worship services at any given hour may become more intimate still. Some of our cavernous worship spaces will need to be downsized for a new era. Some buildings need to be sold, so that churches can start afresh with smaller, more flexible space. An aging cohort of donors will be passing from the scene – meaning that we will have to rethink the ways we choose to spend money.

Facilities and staff strategies have to make sense for the world into which we are moving. Say a doxology for a good yesterday – and a benediction. That was then. This is now. And it's a now chock-full of promise, possibility and the power of God.

I wrote a book about 15 years ago titled *I Refuse to Lead a Dying Church*. This title caught more attention than any other title of any other book I have written. Some people thought it represented a cocky refusal to serve churches that were experiencing ministry decline or that were late in their life cycle. The publisher's graphic artist put a pastor on the cover, which sort of looked like me, with his arms folded defiantly.

But those who got inside those pages discovered just the opposite of disdain for the church late in its life cycle. Refusal to lead a dying church is about embracing the possibilities of today and tomorrow. Dying churches are too often marked by obsessive remembering of the way things used to be, and longing for things to get back to yesterday's style of thriving. Living churches are energized around the challenge of serving God here and now and in the world that is unfolding around them. They are ready to let go of old buildings if necessary, along with dead programs and tired paradigms. They are willing to rethink what they are doing: for a new day and a new context. Often the church that refuses to die chooses to sell its building and walk – but not to close shop. This church chooses to stick together, to discover an identity and a calling that transcends a building, and to pursue a journey with God into a new ministry season.

Buildings can often be re-purposed for a new generation. But I would encourage any church to refuse to consider the subject of selling the old and trading spaces "off the table." A new space may make a lot more sense for the dreams that God is developing among you.

Baseline: the best really is yet to come, if we are open to it.

4. Authenticity is essential – don't try to be something (or somebody) that you are not.

As we will see later in this book, you can always partner with new team members who are more this or more that. You can always start new worship gatherings that are more this or more that. But prioritizing the community's needs in your ministry plan does not mean that you cease worshiping in ways that you find to be deeply life-giving, nor that you let go of any practice that is part of the good stuff that life within your fellowship has historically embraced.

In some cases, the habits and good stuff will continue at one hour or in one venue, but not in another. In other cases, we may choose to share some of the good stuff of our faith tradition with new friends. In my 2019 book *Multi*, I talked about host culture.[1] This is the culture of the faith community that has been around for years in a place.

---

[1] *Multi: The Chemistry of Church Diversity,* Pilgrim Press, 2016, pp. 50-52.

There's nothing gained in trying to be something we are not. There is sometimes much to be gained in discovering constructive ways to share pieces of our tradition with new folks.

- If your church has a long tradition of work in the world of social justice and civil rights – by all means, invite a new generation to come alongside you in that work. Some of their instincts will be different, but you can mentor them none-the-less.

- If your church has a long tradition of powerful music in worship, consider creating a new service with equally powerful, but very different music. Expand your church's range of music, with an eye on the musical language of the community around you. You could sponsor an occasional Gospel Music Night where musicians from varied styles and worship venues come together to share.

- If your church members excel in Korean barbecue, this is something to be savored, literally, with a new generation. Consider passing on the recipes and the tradition to younger church participants and community friends, even if you do not always gather in the same room for worship.

- If Biblical literacy has been a historic value in your Christian education ministry across many years, work with rising leaders to keep this a priority in the years to come. Just understand that the structures and programs for Bible teaching will likely change if this value from the host culture is to be passed along.

- If your church once had the largest youth group in town, you might decide to do a deep-rethink on how you can resource large numbers of youth in the current situation. It likely will no longer be a ministry focused on the children of church members. I work with a church in England that uses a community drama and theater program as their platform for engaging hundreds of young people in constructive relationship and faith formation. Almost none of their parents are members of that church.

- If your church building is adjacent to a university with a heritage of asking questions and thinking deeply about faith – look for ways to pass along this piece of your DNA and ministry, even if it does not happen in church study groups or even in worship.

On the other hand, there will be some places where you and your church friends cannot just appear out of nowhere without seeming really out-of-place, because those places are simply not your place. If you don't ever go to bars, you will be a poor team member for the pub theology ministry.

If you don't share the lifestyle of the target

audience of a particular venue (under-employed young people in one place or old Marines who love to play pool and drink Lone Star in another place) please spare yourself and everyone else the awkwardness. If you don't enjoy reading books to kids, you probably can pass on the children's summer reading ministry.

If you really don't have a passion for a group's cause, then you could find yourself using the group for a purpose totally un-related to why the group exists – which is recruiting for another cause. If you are not already online and active in multiple platforms, it never hurts to become more technologically savvy – but TikTok may just not be your thing. Don't force it.

There are people who are cut out perfectly to build relationships and even develop influence in each of these places. You may want to strategically partner with folks who can authentically go where you cannot. More about this in the pages ahead.

Baseline: God wants us to be ourselves.

5. No church can serve everybody – so each church had better get focused on particular somebodies.

Your church's main worship service(s) may authentically express your foundational beliefs and ways of living out faith. It may be that with modest adjustments, new persons can be effectively grafted into the worship community now existing. But even if they cannot be, there is value in continuing to worship in ways that are deeply authentic to your church's identity, culture and understanding.

But, whether you seek to graft new people into your current gatherings or to create parallel ministry gatherings for new people, you have to have somebody in mind in order to design ministry. The more generic a church feels, the less interesting and compelling it will be. The church designed to work for everybody engages almost nobody these days.

- Find a people niche or two, and focus.

- Working parents trying to raise great children.

- People who got a good dose of Jesus early in life, but have been burned by fundamentalist religion along the way.

- People from the big city who are moving into a rural zip code.

- The young adult children of first generation African immigrants, who may have attended immigrant churches in North America up through their teens, but who now find themselves in a spiritual no-one's land.

- People who work with a computer screen in their faces 50 hours or more a week, and who long to be with warm bodies, far from a screen, in a multi-sensory experience with food, sound and touch.

- People who (on the contrary) would rather pop on to their home Wi-Fi as their primary gateway for worship and exploration of faith, than to get dressed, travel across town, make small talk with strangers, and figure out lunch afterwards.

- LGBTQ couples and their kids who would love to find a church family.

- People who are in recovery from addiction.

- Ex-Catholics with strong reasons for leaving, but who miss certain vestiges of their church experience.

- Families that are struggling to survive financially and to find enough food each month.

- People who work all week in order to spend Saturday and Sunday in the great outdoors. (Why would we try to lure them indoors during prime recreational time?)

- People who are deeply into the local music scene, going to local concerts and/or performing in a local group.

- Military families who have moved into the community, and who will likely last three or four years before moving to another city.

- Young retirees from the upper Midwest.

- Christian parents who want their children's faith formation to happen in a place with progressive Christian values.

- People who spend a lot of time on golf courses and/ or tennis courts.

RECOMMENDED TOOL: MISSION INSITE

The most widely used computer-based tool for understanding community demographics for ministry in the United States is Mission Insite. They produce some outstanding products that can help you better understand the many people groups that come together to form your neighborhood, your city or your region. When you run a basic report on a prescribed geographical area, you will get information on what Mosaic Lifestyle Groups make up your area's distinctive population mix. These groups are sorted by the ways they spend money (or not). Good research has been done on how they each differ one from the next, and how each invites a slightly (or radically) different ministry approach. Find out the major Mosaic Lifestyle Groups in your church's ministry zone. If you like, plot your church participants by address, so that you can see what Lifestyle Groups your church specializes in already. Mission Insite reveals ministry preferences that differ from one community to the next, due to the mix of people. You may discover that your church is doing things that are driving away the very folks you are trying to gather, and see ways you could improve. Your regional denominational office probably has a Mission Insite contract.

www.missioninsite.com

Baseline: The more clarity you have about the kinds of people that you are designing your ministry for, the better.

6. Friendship first, then ministry development.

When the people inside the church start plotting what to do for the people outside the church, a bad church meeting is underway. If you are reading this book, chances are good you have been in that meeting at least once. There is no way that a group of folks, long on the inside, disconnected to some degree from the cultural currents all around them, can design ministry for people on the outside. Can't be done. I have been saying so in leader seminars for many years.

So people go home from the seminars, determined to convene focus groups or develop a new launch team among the population that they wish to reach. But they have trouble finding anyone who will sit down with them to work on this. So the next time I talk to them they complain about the people they are seeking to engage. "The neighbors won't engage." "They don't care." "They're on drugs." "They are just more interested in other things, community sports, etc." I have heard it all.

In fact, the people we want to design ministry for may not be actively looking for a church in their life, much less to try to plant and organize one from scratch. So, we go back to the bad church meeting where we try to read their minds in their absence. Or we give up.

Let's step back for a moment and think on this. If our church is somewhat disconnected from a certain population, we might should become more engaged with them before trying to develop a worship service or a formal ministry with them. In dating terms, we don't go out once, and then start planning a wedding – it's too much too fast. We don't know each other yet. There is no trust yet, no shared history. No friendship.

Friendships develop in spaces where all parties share interest or feel at home. Where is such a space in your neighborhood, where some of the people in your church can begin to forge friendship with the people you would love to engage in ministry?

- Recovery groups. The point is recovery, and friendship arises from that shared agenda. Note: recovery groups are not appropriate settings for all-out church recruiting.
- Community-focused task groups, working together for a certain end: a justice issue, a political issue, developing a new park or community service,

helping neighbors attain English proficiency and literacy.

- Recreation and Common interests. When the apartheid system collapsed and Nelson Mandela became president of South Africa, the nation teetered on the verge of civil war. They used community soccer to throw diverse young people together on a playing field and develop friendship muscles that could then be used in a new effort of post-colonial nation building.

- Dog parks and public swimming pools are great places where neighbors show up at similar times and similar days – and friendships grow. More than once in my work with church planters, we have observed that the neighborhood needs to be planted first before we can even begin trying to plant a church.

- The Dairy Queen (in small town Oklahoma) or the corner pub (in many cities), where the same crew shows up day after day and become truly neighbors.

How often I have watched when persons working on a new ministry launch were part of a team responsible for some facet of the ministry – children or hospitality, for example. They reach out to their real-live friends and recruit them to help. We are talking real-live human beings they enjoy being with: people they've worked with, volunteered with and gone to the beach with. Often these are friends who don't go to church at all.

So they say, "I am on a team, working on a new faith community – it's a new church, but different in a lot of ways from the existing churches (and they explain the core vision of how it's fresh or distinctive). I know you are not really a church person, but my team is working with the kids – and you're amazing with kids. Would you be willing to help me out with this as we get started?"

And very often, the answer is, "Sure." And if it's a maybe, when we are talking to friends, the conversation keeps going: "Would you give it three weeks? I gave you three weeks when you were running the community barbecue for the sports association."

Friends have history. And relationship can be very persuasive.

RECOMMENDED TOOL: IDI

The Intercultural Development Inventory is a powerful tool, used by all sorts of organizations, including faith communities. For persons in your church who are serious about improving your skills for intercultural friendship and partnership, this is an online inventory that will reveal where you are personally in terms of your likely effectiveness, your internal anxiety, appropriate good manners and healthy authenticity in cross-cultural situations.

For more information: www.iciinventory.com

As of this writing, several persons on the Path 1 Team at Discipleship Ministries are trained in using IDI with church leaders. There are also plenty of regional judicatory leaders around the country who are similarly trained. Ask around, and you may find persons who can help your group process the learning from IDI toward increased effectiveness in developing friendships and collaboration between your church and your community.

Baseline: Jesus was good at making friends outside his demographic. John chapter 4 is a good case in point.

7. Cultural competency requires spiritual readiness

About ten years ago, Christie Latona and I sought to create a way to measure a church's readiness for stepping outside its comfort zone for the sake of its mission. It began as we puzzled over this question: *Why do some churches seem to enjoy the challenge of starting new gatherings and places for new people, and others (if they try) are likely to sabotage the new ministry in order to protect the existing church?* We studied churches that seemed to thrive in their efforts to create ministry for a wider circle of people – in North America and in Asia. And the Readiness 360 project was born. Four broad themes emerged to characterize the most effective churches, each of which we seek to evaluate:

- Spiritual intensity – people in these churches experienced the presence of God in their lives and in their common life.

- Missional alignment – these churches were able to prioritize activities and investments that clearly advanced the mission.

- Dynamic relationships – these churches had good relational habits both within their fellowship and between the church and their neighbors.

- Cultural openness – these churches were able to cross certain boundaries of human diversity effectively.

RECOMMENDED TOOL: R360

Readiness 360 involves a customized survey that you give to your church participants. It yields a detailed report that will help you assess both the spiritual energy and the cross-cultural experience that you have on your team. For a reasonable price, you get a detailed report with leader tips. See **www.readiness360.org**. Your conference or denomination may already have a contract with R360. Check and see – but you can also purchase the tool online independently.

When we speak of a church's "cultural competency," we are looking at the fourth theme above, along with some of the relationship habits and ingrained good manners from the third.

As we worked with hundreds of congregations taking the inventory, we discovered something. One of the four themes, as it strengthened, would raise capacity in the other four areas. As spiritual intensity increased, other areas tended to strengthen as well. This was a surprise to us – and then, as we thought about it more, not surprising at all.

We as Christians have long known that the Holy Spirit has the power to drive changes in the human heart that transcends all the educating and organizing that we can do. The much-loved hymn "Amazing Grace" speaks to a slave trader's encounter with God's love that in turn enabled him to truly look in the mirror and see himself honestly in terms of the horrors he had perpetuated. He writes of grace that could "save a wretch like me." The term, wretch, has been criticized in modern times because it conjured up too negative a view of human nature. But, slave trading is awfully wretched. Racism is wretched. I am not sure the words are too strong at all. Human beings can go pretty low, and our behaviors and attitudes can create enormous pain and difficulties in the lives of others, especially others whom we live apart from.

Many of us know from dealing with racism in the church, that sometimes we remove it funeral by funeral. Racism roots itself so deep in an individual, so that they may hold on to their views and privilege stubbornly, until death. And when their church is no longer a place where they can safely speak in racist ways, they just go quiet at church. And their racism comes out in other ways, often politically.

But, encounters with the Holy Spirit can do spiritual surgery that goes equally deep within us. When a group of people seriously seek God-encounter in their lives, all kinds of change become possible. One needed change for the church seeking an expanded ministry field is a shift from thinking about our church possessively to thinking about it generously – as a gift to be shared with others, even at the risk of losing certain aspects of church life that have grown comfortable for us.

RECOMMENDED TOOLS:

A small-group experience may gently warm people up in terms of exploring the spiritual quest together. One excellent small-group experience is **UNBINDING THE GOSPEL**[2] – this resource is designed to help church people get more comfortable talking about faith, and not just the weather and church gossip. Given the intensity of many people's schedules, it is easier to block out a weekend than one night every week. A retreat may be a better option, one such as **WALK TO EMMAUS**[3] a weekend short course on Christianity that focuses on cultivating, in some cases birthing, a personal relationship with God. And, of course, **VOLUNTEER MISSION SERVICE**, either in one's community or on a trip to a distant place, specifically where participants have the opportunity to serve poor people and to build relationships with poor people. Volunteering with a public school, an ESL class, a food ministry, a home-repair project – experiences serving others are often spiritually transformative – especially when there is direct personal interaction with the population served.

Baseline: A robust inward expedition makes for a better outward expedition.

[2] Martha Grace Reese and Brian McLaren, *Unbinding the Gospel,* 2nd Edition, 2018.

[3] www.emmaus.upperroom.org

8. Social privilege often gets in our way.

One of the more joyful ministry experiences in my life was a community children's ministry in a small town. Our church had only half a dozen kids in Sunday school and the age gaps were such that everyone was miserable. We needed more children for it to work. So we created a Wednesday night fellowship with around 50 children – which reached across income segments and also may have been one of the earliest joining of Black children and White children in faith community in that town's history. (For a church with 90 worshipers on Sunday, this was a big deal.) We even managed to get the parents all together in one room if their children were performing – but it was very hard to move the parents from that experience to further engagement with our church.

And the trouble was this: our church members had the most education and probably the highest per capita income of any church in the community. We were that church. I drove pretty low-end cars at that point in life, so even I as pastor was aware that one had to cross a wall of Mercedes, Cadillacs and BMWs to get into our church building on a Sunday.

And once you got inside, most people were wearing the latest fashions of clothing, often bought this season from the best stores. If you hung around a bit longer, you might discover that our church practically owned the country club in town – I am guessing that forty percent of our folks were members there, too. You get the picture. We were that church in our community – and our relative social privilege created an invisible barrier for most of our neighbors.

And, of course, social privilege does not simply exist in terms of money. There is also race – and this aspect of privilege is in even harder to address. If any of the following scenarios are true, a church could be walking into a minefield of challenge in terms of becoming multi-ethnic:

- **The leadership in the church is significantly whiter than the church participants or the folks who live around the church building. This church may excel in organizing a helping ministry of some sort (food pantry, free store, etc.), but a lot of people will have difficulty fully trusting the church, and even more difficulty choosing to attend a church gathering.**

- **A White or affluent church is new to a neighborhood that has historically been home to people of color,** and populated mostly by people who commute in on Sunday or who have moved into the neighborhood quite recently. Some neighbors may perceive this new church as having a savior complex. Others may see hints of White Christian colonialism.

• The church has made some inroads into collecting a multi-ethnic cast of leaders, but the power is still imbalanced between persons of various races in terms of ministry ideas or the way that issues of race and/or social injustice are framed and addressed. White perspectives still dominate in ways both obvious and subtle. Frank and ongoing conversation about White privilege and anti-racism will be needed if the ministry team is to reach its potential.

Reading a single book or attending a seminar is not enough to eliminate this kind of challenge to effective ministry. Tackling racial privilege requires steadily growing awareness and ongoing commitment to learn more about ourselves, to discover how insidious racism is, and to acknowledge how deeply it has soaked into our common life. Unless a multi-racial community is committed to work on this together, healing and discipleship will be disrupted.

The church leader team that chooses to brush off the challenges of social privilege and racial privilege will significantly limit their options as they consider the ministry strategies in the latter part of this book.

Baseline: We white guys, in particular, have some personal work to do if we want to be a part of Pentecost-energy ministry!

RECOMMENDED TOOLS:

Urban Village Church in Chicago (a faith community that I deeply admire) has worked with Crossroads Antiracism (**www.crossroadsantiracism.org**) over an 18-month time frame for both a church audit and coaching. According to pastor Emily McGinley, they have trained leaders within their church to help church participants "identify and dismantle the ways that Internal Racial Superiority/Oppression are taking shape within them." Study groups have considered a whole range of helpful books including *How to be an Anti-Racist* (Ibram Kendi), *Minor Feelings* (Cathy Park Hong), *White Fragility* (Robin DiAngelo), *The New Jim Crow* (Michelle Alexander), *The Thoughtful Christian's Anti-Racism study packet and A People's History of the United States* (Howard Zinn). For Urban Village, this kind of work is at the heart of Christian discipleship.

9. Community partnerships are priceless.

- Look for people, especially beyond your church, who are engaged in ministry and action for good in your ministry zone. Look for people who care about your community. Join forces.

- The benefits of community partnerships are almost too long to list here.

- It's less work up front: We don't always have to organize something ourselves. We can show up to someone else's party if we believe in what its about.

- Friendship and relationships in the neighborhood can grow exponentially, both with newfound co-workers in a partnership and with those who may be beneficiaries or served. Through such relationships and experiences, we can really come to understand our community in a deeper way.

- Even if only a few of our church folks are available and willing to show up in this partnership, it still connects our church to important work in the neighborhood.

- In fact, by dividing up our church representatives among several community mission initiatives, we gain a wider experience of our community. If we have 20 people volunteering in half a dozen community organizations or initiatives, and they come back to compare notes and share what they are learning – our church gains powerful missional wisdom.

- We may discover a particular community partner

that offers a gateway for endless community service possibilities: a nearby public school could be such a partner, especially if we demonstrate that we are trustworthy and that we will not take advantage of service contact time to recruit for church activities.

- From friendships and immersion in community, great new ministry ideas may emerge – and the best ones will often come from our neighbors. I know two free stores that birthed new churches – one in a big city and one in a rural community in Virginia. But it happened organically in both cases, with the development of genuine friendships becoming the link between the social service ministry and the birth of a new faith community.

- Such partnerships are often a good use of church buildings. Years ago when Amy Butler was the pastor at Calvary Baptist, down the street from our home in Washington DC, she looked for directors of community organizations that she really liked as human beings, persons where she felt synergy. She would invite such organizations to share space in Calvary's building. In turn, Calvary got much more than building rent – they got a staff of partners who could meet regularly and talk about how to advance the Reign of God in the city. The church showed up for the ministries of the partners, and the partners showed up at times for ministries sponsored by the church.

Baseline: Collect some allies and partners.

10. Good listening may lead to un-learning, which leads to even better listening.

Preconceived notions and stereotypes can really throw us off. Things that were true yesterday, and may not be true today, can trip us up. Even if we have lived in the same neighborhood for decades, we may be surprised to discover more closely the experiences and values of the neighbors we don't hang out with: the younger set, the new-comers, the people who speak a different language. We may need to un-learn some ideas that are incorrect and that are blocking us from engaging with these neighbors constructively.

One great exercise in getting started listening and un-learning is a **prayer walk**. We meet at the church or at a coffee shop and go out into the neighborhood to walk around for an hour, with the prayer on your heart, "God, please show me something I need to see in order to better understand my neighbors." We deliberately suspend all assumptions and just look with curiosity. The family in the first house you pass has tall weeds in their yard. Your easy assumption could be, "These people don't care enough to mow their grass."

A better stance is to say, "I wonder why the grass is so high here." We might be surprised by the amount of care in that home. It might be that they can't afford a lawn mower or that they work multiple shifts to put food on the table and have no energy left for yard work. Or you might say, "In the lives of this family, I bet there are things a lot more important than these weeds. I wonder what they are."

An alternative to a prayer walk is to sit on a park bench and **write love letters to people**. We just people watch until someone catches our eye, and then write them a letter (which they will never read) sharing what we wish we could say to them related to the Christian Good News if we knew them. This exercise forces us to look more closely, to really see people, and to nurture compassion for them.

Best of all are **1:1 conversations**, where we invite people that seem interesting (and have a pulse) to give us half an hour and to tell us about themselves. The 1:1 meeting is a precious tool from the community-organizing world. This kind of encounter is not to advertise our ministry – but to discover what they the other can teach us, to discover what energizes them. There is no hard agenda to the conversation, no clipboard with set questions. We allow the conversation to flow where it flows. When people tell us something interesting, we stop and ask why. Paying attention to their energy and emotion, to their humor, to what seems important to them, these conversations are ever surprising.

It is a conversation, so we should be reciprocal. But we don't have a lot of time, so it's best to avoid over-sharing about oneself. A good goal is to keep it to where the other person gets 70 percent of the airtime. This is about powerful, focused listening. Best we not take notes – we can write down what we remember afterwards. And if the conversation gets boring or tedious, then we should interrupt them to ask something more personal – to get them talking more personally. A 30-minute conversation might go like this in places:

- "Our church is really in a listening mode, trying to pay attention to what's going on in people's lives, so that we can create programs and organize ministry that is relevant and helpful. I would love to pick your brain, hear a little of your story and your angle on this community. Would you have a half an hour to chat?"

- "So what brought you to live here? What do you think? Why did you choose here, or did here choose you? What's really good about living here? What's hard about life here? (If the person has children) Where do your kids go to school? You like the school?" Etc.

- "Tell me what I might be missing when I look around in this neighborhood. Where do you think my church or I need to pay close attention?"

- "What kind of work you do? Tell me about something you love to do, or that you are good at. How did you get good at it? Did someone teach you to love this thing, or mentor you at it? Are there other people around here who share your passion? Do you get together with them? What happens? Or if you were to get together with them, what might happen?"

- "What experiences or special people helped make you who you are? (Let's say the person's name is Malcolm.) How did you get to be this Malcolm?"

- Toward the end of the half hour, we can share just a bit about whatever our church is up to in the community or about how we got involved with it." (Let's keep this part very brief, unless they riddle you with questions.)

- After 30 minutes, we wrap it up. Forty minutes is the absolute stop – at this point we apologize that we have to run. We thank them for their time. We probably did not make it through half the things we could have explored in such a short conversation. So we can decide on the spot if we would like to spend another half hour with this person in the near future. If we would like to visit again, we should ask them if that would be okay. We tell them honestly if and how their story has been helpful or encouraging for us. And whenever possible, we ask: "Is there someone else in our community that I should talk to? You've heard a bit about what we are up to. Is there someone who comes to mind who might have insight we need to hear?"

RECOMMENDED TOOLS:

Pick your favorite search engine and look up "community organizing relational meeting." You will find several good **YOUTUBE VIDEOS** that explain and demonstrate the nature of this kind of interaction.

Also I recommend the book by my friend and previous co-author Beth Ann Estock, titled simply **DISCERNMENT**.[4] It is not a long read, and it can help both individuals and teams turn off the tape player and shed assumptions in order to see and hear more clearly.

---

[4]   Beth Ann Estock, *Discernment,* Abingdon Press, 2019.

11. A lot of what we try will go about as well as a Wile E. Coyote scheme.

I am old just enough to remember the first Roadrunner cartoon on CBS. I was there, up early in my pajamas on Saturday morning, September 10, 1966. Granted I was four years old. (So I had to go back to look up the date.) The TV commercials on CBS late that summer had built up the new Saturday morning cartoon line-up. I got up early that September Saturday to watch them all. I guess my parents were asleep in bed. It was just me, a box of Fruit Loops and a black and white TV. When the Roadrunner came on, I remember there was no dialogue. Just beep-beep. And yet I was transfixed. Even today, when I am exhausted from a tough day of work even today, there is nothing better than a dose of the Road Runner and Wile E. Coyote to help me unwind.

This cartoon is an endless variation of a coyote plotting to catch a roadrunner. But he never does. "Wile E. Coyote, super genius" the coyote would say to himself: with plots becoming increasingly fantastical, involving elaborate mechanisms with giant anvils and TNT. Yet, every time, Roadrunner darts by too fast, and the trap ends up backfiring on the coyote. So, the mention of a Wile E. Coyote scheme becomes shorthand for a plan that falls flat. Hopefully it falls flat without exploding.

Whenever we are creating a new ministry, we are trying something new with a group of people. Even if what we are attempting may have worked perfectly with another group of people, chances are that these people have not talked at all to those people. So there is always a little suspense whether a new ministry attempt will be a break-through or will end with a coyote falling into the Grand Canyon. And, as often as not, it is the latter. Sometimes, the idea itself was great, but we failed to do the people networking up front. Other times, the new ministry needs to be tweaked a bit. I shared in an earlier chapter about a community children's ministry my church launched in a small town that was a total hit. I failed to mention an earlier attempt that attracted only two sisters and no other children at all.

We just don't often hit the bulls-eye on the first try – or if we do (grace and beginners luck in symphony), the second try is liable to be a dud. And we wonder what happened. This is normal.

So, it's a good idea to play with a ministry idea or aspects of it for a while. Try one-off events. See if the events engage new participants. Or do a very short series, with a clear end-point. Discover why people like it, and what could make it better. Then you can launch it weekly after that.

But, baseline: Sometimes you will strike out.

12. God is alive and at work in every neighborhood. Our challenge is to show up to what God is doing.

One good reason for prayer-walking and 1:1 conversations is to help us discover clues as to what God is up to already all around us. Once we discern things under way that align with what we know of God, the next challenge is to show up to those trends, to those projects, to those populations that are engaged with whatever is going on. Getting connected with the people who are already caught up in a God-thing is critical.

If I am trying to start a new ministry, I want the perspective and influence of such people on my team. I want their connection to others. And, where possible, I want my team to build upon the foundation of whatever good is currently unfolding.

In looking for the places where God is at work – we can start by examining the strong institutions that exist in our community. When I was planting a second campus of a church, our team looked around and discovered these community assets already in play:

- One of the best regional hospitals in the country, right in the middle of town. Not only were there great professionals associated with this hospital; but, they were well-trained in a culture of organizational excellence and service hospitality.

- A strong elementary school just a couple miles from our new location. We had amazing educators among us.

- A community youth sports program that had overgrown the capacity of county facilities. Between the school and sports program, this community was turning out highly capable young people, with leadership potential far beyond.

- A robust network of 12-step recovery programs addressing a variety of addictions.

The hospital community of medical professionals mostly remained with the mother campus of our church. But teachers from the local elementary school were on our launch team, and they reached other teachers. This was a critical asset as we began to reach families from that school. There was no direct evangelism at that public school. But the families that loved Oriole Beach Elementary School discovered a similar winsome vibe at our church. Those teachers brought that. And word spread fast. We capitalized on the community's appreciation for youth sports by creating parallel leagues with the sports association's leagues – seeking to complement what they did, not to compete. We found parents and others eager to jump in to coach and lead – their commitment to the value of youth sports was already in place. And we offered free space in our building to several recovery circles that were ready to multiply. In each case, community people brought strength to our ministry – values and skills already in place, along with strong relational networks.

As you and your team survey the landscape in your church's mission zone, some things to ask:

- What in this community is legendary on the community grapevine? Where do we see excellence?
- Who is investing in children?

- Who is investing in meeting human needs? Look
  for the movers and the shakers – but also look
  for people who have worked with them, been
  mentored by them to some degree and fallen
  under their good influence.

- What else has started and thrived in the last few
  years? Where is the start-up energy? Why has the
  thing thrived and grown? Who is in charge? How
  are they networking and developing their good
  thing? This could be a community initiative or a
  private company. It could be another church.

  A good start-up is almost always a great community
  asset. Even if the start up is a gang or deals in drugs
  – one significant conversion to faith within a well-
  networked organization and you might have a great
  local leader on your hands ready to put their know-
  how to work for God.

Baseline: Show up to what God is doing.

13. Regardless of strategy, spiritual collaboration with new people is essential.

In the final section of this book (just ahead)
we will review a few of the basic strategies
for how existing ministries can relate to new
ministries. I have never seen a church revitalized

or transformed without the start of new ministry initiatives within and around the ministry. So it is important that we explore varied ways that churches anchor and connect to God's new things in the neighborhood.

But regardless of the strategy that is right for our church, spiritual collaboration is a non-negotiable. Existing churches cannot plant new things by themselves, unless they are planting the new ministry only to reach the exact same kind of people who are already engaged in their ministry. Sometimes a ministry fills its space quickly with pent-up demand for more space for more people to engage in exactly the same thing that the church is already doing. In that case, we can take fifty or a hundred people from the room that is filled to overflowing, go five miles away and do exactly the same thing we were doing, and it may take root and thrive almost immediately – if the people in the new neighborhood look like the launch team that we recruited from the existing church.

However, most of the time, we are going to need some of our neighbors to help us. It works like this: the first 200 people will look a lot like the first 40. As the ministry grows, it will diversify in unpredictable ways. But if we are seeking to reach a certain set of people, who are not currently represented in our congregation, we need that kind of people on the start-up team. Half the churches I work with try to take short cuts on this. This invariably leads to disappointment.

I understand that sometimes it is hard to diversify a ministry launch team – in which case, I would encourage a church to slow down and build the relationships. Develop the trust around the table, so that the team not only looks like the community they are setting out to engage, but they think like them also. And they have relational connections, so that inviting can happen naturally.

Any collaboration with local people is a good thing – but the best collaboration is spiritual. It is where we begin to pray together about the community, and the emerging ministry. In such a spiritual collaboration, amazing things begin to happen.

Just as disappointment almost always follows

the team that fails to incorporate appropriate diversity (mirroring the people they seek to reach), there is a corollary happy truth: when a diverse circle of leaders are praying their way into their new ministry, the ministry almost never fails to take root.

If there are people on our team, who:

- **Represent the demographic that you seek to reach,**

- **And they have been disengaged from church in the neighborhood (out of boredom, busyness or whatever)**

- **And they have recently experienced some kind of personal spiritual awakening,**

then our team is in for a God-surprise. We have spiritual energy and missional wisdom. We have people with fresh God experience, fresh enough to actually tell someone about it and about the new ministry the are excited about. We have people that will actually invite others. And we have people who, when things get too churchy or too (whatever), will tell us to go easy.

Baseline: Indigenous spiritual collaborators are priceless.

RANKING BASELINES:

Before we get into the Strategies section, page back through the thirteen baselines that I have shared. For convenience, there is a list of them on page 16. Rank them according to the urgency that you see they present to your church's leader team and/or to the new ministry team that you seek to develop. I have not presented them in any particular ranking of importance – because that will vary with each church. But you can rank them.

If it is something critical that your team needs to hear early in the work, rank it high. If it is something that you already know and/or practice in your church, rank it lower. You may invite your whole team to read this book – but you as leaders will have to decide where to slow down and really let something sink in.

Which baselines rank highest and most urgent in your context? As you develop your M.A.P, this list will be important. Dog-ear this page.

1.

2.

3.

4.

5.

6.

Strategies and Your Church's Ministry Expedition

All of the baselines are directly relevant to a church's ministry planning. You have assessed that some are more urgent in your context than others. Now we move to strategies. In this case, you can only pick one. It might be that you could see two or three of the strategies working well in your context. You may combine two in some way. But ultimately, you can't pursue every strategy. Your church's expedition toward renewed ministry can't head in every direction. Finally, your church's Expedition Team will have to choose its strategy. Both in this choice and in the journey to follow, an Expedition Guide and/or a seasoned ministry coach will be invaluable.

One of my favorite books is *The River of Doubt*

by Candice Millard.[5] This book tells the story of Teddy Roosevelt's mid-life crisis after he was done being President of the United States. He craved one more great adventure. So he, one of his sons and a group of friends decided to make an expedition deep into the Amazon and discover a new river or something. They discovered that new river as well as disease and local folks who were less than happy to see them. Quickly, it became clear that what seemed like a romantic adventure when imagined from the United States was in fact an ill-advised journey into danger, dis-orientation and (for some in the party) death. The moral of that story – an expedition is a usually lot more joyful when we have someone with us who knows the territory, advising us and re-directing us when we move into a danger zone. Another moral to that story – your church's boredom, dissatisfaction with its status quo or romantic longing for the action of years gone by is not going to be enough to sustain you on a bold ministry expedition into the 2020s. There had best be something (Someone) greater than any of that driving you!

---

5   Candice Millard, *The River of Doubt: Theodore Roosevelt's Darkest Journey,* New York: Broadway Books, 2009.

As your church settles on a strategy, it may be tempting to simply list pros and cons as we would do with a business decision. But in this case, with the church, we are working with God's business! After all the networking and the research, prayer is key. Refer back to Baseline twelve.

RECOMMENDED TOOLS:

We have referenced each of these earlier. Whichever strategy you pursue, (1) my 2019 book *Multi: The Chemistry of Church Diversity* is designed to help teams thrive in diversity. (2) *The Intercultural Development Inventory* is worthwhile for helping all kinds of people strengthen their skills and self-awareness for navigating relationships with diverse people. (3) *Readiness 360* offers a wider participation at a very low per person cost, with a detailed report back to the church. And finally, (4) do you have an Expedition Guide or a ministry coach to come with you on the journey ahead?

We do not have the space here to get into details and teach excellence and how-to for any of the following strategies. This consideration of strategies is more for the purpose of assessing the possibilities of each for your church, given certain variables.

After you have prayed, consulted with your

guide or coach and settled on a particular strategy, then your team can go deeper into understanding how to pursue it with excellence.

1. **Growing a launch team that bridges the church with some community folks (indigenous) and then starting a new worship community.**

I list this one first because it is typically the first thing that churches consider. "Lets take some of our people who are (fill in the blank) and work with them in creating a ministry that will relate well to their peers and friends." The heart of this strategy is taking people whom we believe can build bridges between the church and the community, and empowering them to build such a ministry bridge.

This strategy might be right for your church if:

- Your church has a good group of people who represent the demographic you would like to see more of.

- You are able to reach beyond that group of people (who are now very much insider to your church) to engage people who are outsiders to your church early in the development of the launch team.

- The people on the launch team have a good relationship and history with the existing church. No lingering bitterness.

- You suspect that the per capita financial donations from the new ministry participants may lag in the early years.

- Your current church leadership is willing to allow this ministry to differ in certain ways from the existing ministry. While there will be good common values between this new ministry and the rest of the church, your leaders understand that it must differ in certain ways. An example might be the way you organize and teach financial stewardship or how you practice hospitality. Different systems and strategies may be in order for different populations and generations.

- You are prepared to deal with the challenges that would accompany a new ministry's success – specifically if it were to outgrow the rest of the church or to develop in ways that eventually might lead to the new ministry "leaving home" and forming a new church organizationally. When ministries succeed wildly, sometimes they will grow to renew and change the DNA of the existing church. Other times they will grow up and need to leave the nest. Is your leader team prepared to deal with such good problems?

- Your church's *Readiness 360* report reveals a composite readiness index of 310 or higher.[6]

---

[6] The composite readiness index is simply the sum of the readiness number attached to each of the four readiness components (spirituality, relationships, alignment, openness).

This strategy might be challenging for your church if:

- There are major differences between the socio-economics of the new ministry participants and that of existing church members. Or there is any other dynamic that might intimidate the new people, especially if we are basing the new ministry in the existing church building.

- A significant number of the current church members are ambivalent or annoyed by the new ministry, so that territorial behavior might emerge (not sharing supplies or treating the new people like outsiders rather than family).

- Your leaders are unwilling to allow new leaders to arise and to take the appropriate lead in decisions related to the new ministry and/or worship community. (This will result in the new ministry plateauing in its growth far below its potential.)

- The core of the church members that you have tagged to seed the launch team are internally focused, content with church as it exists, and/or lacking interest or skills for reaching new people. They may have been together as a group of friends within the church for years, with deep interpersonal relationship. We sometimes find that the remnant of young adults in a traditional church are more comfortable with the ways of the older folks at the church and may seek to block the kinds of changes that would make the church more engaging to their peers. Remember: the most typical younger Americans have dis-engaged from church participation since age 15. The remnant of younger churchgoers is often decidedly different from their peers. Counting on them to build an effective ministry bridge may be unrealistic.

2. Creating a safe space for the birth of a new faith community, that is distinctive from your church – but very much a partner in ministry.

You may share facilities with the new faith community – but even if not, you share a mission zone. And you want to help one another succeed. But you are thinking big picture, beyond the long-term survival of your church. You care deeply about keeping a strong Christian witness in your community, possibly based from your church property. So you partner with an emerging ministry, possibly offering free office space and meeting space. You may take an occasional offering to support the new ministry. Your partnership might also entail being ready to robustly defend the new ministry and to seek to block anything or anybody who would get in their way, possibly including a few of your own church members. If you have a large facility with multiple meeting spaces, you may seek to collect partner congregations and to transition the facility from a single church facility to a ministry center and collaborative, even possibly developing a partnership advisory board that thinks big picture related to the neighborhood.

This strategy might be right for your church if:

- You have very few of the kinds of people you are seeking to reach already active within your church.

- You have been able to identify Christian leaders that you believe would be pleasant to partner with. These could be from within your denomination or not.

- You are able to establish a clear covenant between your church and the new church, including issues of space sharing, defraying costs (such as cleaning and utilities), with a clear end date. The end date insures that the relationship can be reviewed regularly and adjusted as needed.

- There is reasonable openness from the new church for defined partnership in mission: that could range from helping people with needs in the community to occasional joint worship or fellowship events. If they have more children than your church, a joint children's ministry event might be ideal. But they will have to be open to this.

- Holding on to your facility is important to you but without a sharing of costs, it will not be possible.

This strategy might be challenging for your church if...

- Your leaders really long to change your own church's ministry trajectory, and would rather focus on birthing a new ministry connected to your current church organization, perhaps as the church that will carry your ministry legacy forward.

- You haven't yet had the critical conversations to name your church's vision and how partnering with this new ministry advances that vision.

- Your church's Readiness 360 report reveals a composite readiness index of 295 or below. This would indicate that many of your people would likely find the presence of another church among you to be annoying – or at best, un-interesting.

- You can't find a partner that seems a good fit, for whatever reason.

3. **Partnering with another church that is well rooted with another constituency, possibly a different generation, ethnicity or mother tongue.**

This strategy is similar to number two, except it envisions even less direct collaboration between the existing church members and the new ministry.

The two churches can still share occasional worship, fellowship or mission experiences. Or not. Over-sharing is not necessarily going to be helpful. The young church needs to be free to do what it takes to reach its focus population, without using up limited time and energy to plan joint projects with the partner church. Where there is sharing from one church to the next, it might entail just a few staff or leaders, rather than the entire congregations.

This strategy might be right for your church if:

- The demographic changes in your neighborhood are so significant or your median age is now so advanced that your congregation now foresees a limited life expectancy for itself.

- The new group clearly has a better chance of growing ministry.

- By cost sharing with other congregations, your congregation can pay basic bills and survive a few more years.

- Depending on certain variables, you could keep options open in terms of how the building might be passed along to the new group as your church comes to the end of its run.

- Your church unreservedly feels good and supportive of the new ministry – even if it is clearly designed for people with different instincts and culture. You can feel good that your church is stewarding its building to bless this new church and, in turn, to bless your community neighbors.

- Your church's *Readiness 360* report indicates a composite readiness index that is under 295, making it quite challenging for your church to pursue a more direct pathway to ministry renewal.

This strategy might be challenging for your church if...

- Your leaders long deep in their hearts for your church to do more. So strategies one and two just get your blood pumping with more hope.

- Or, on the opposite end of the possibility spectrum, you sense it is really getting time to talk about bringing the current church's life to a conclusion and thinking about legacy. In this case, why get tied up in leases to outside groups or churches? You may want to tend to the questions of legacy first (Strategies four and five).

- You would like to explore divesting of the current facility and possibly leaving the current neighbor-hood: relocating to plant your church fresh with a new team in another part of your city or region (Strategy six). In this case, getting the property ready to sell is priority. Occasionally, a group that is renting space may become the buyer of the property – but usually not.

4. Merging with a church whose core population is younger than yours and increasing within the geographic area.

Mergers are tricky.

So you want to get married. You now have to find someone you want to marry and live with. In the summer of 2020, during the height of the Covid-19 Pandemic, when it seemed the whole world was binge watching on Netflix and Amazon, a new TV reality show blew through titled "Indian Matchmaking." The show featured this real-live matchmaker from Mumbai who would often travel to the USA to present South Asian families with candidates for their grown children to marry. It was typical reality TV, with lots of drama and awkwardness. Some couples seemed to stick, others not.

But after the first season, an investigation revealed that every single couple paired by the matchmaker had in fact broken up before their marriage. This was even true of the couples in India.

Apparently, times are a changing in the world of relationships for south Asian culture. And 21st century people in almost all cultures are picky about who they marry. Divorce rates are rising in India, because spouses refuse to put up with what they used to put up with. Marriage is challenging.

This is true with church mergers as well. They typically don't work as advertised or as hoped. Something like this can happen:

- Both of the merging churches were advanced in median age and declining, and their decline continues unabated after they merge. They buy themselves five or ten years, and then they face survival challenges once again.

- One of the merging churches was younger. Its energy and style (maybe different worship culture) thrives, and the ministry has grown. Within five years, there is a good ministry legacy but almost no one from the older church is left – and this can be a great outcome for ministry in the neighborhood – but maybe not quite what people imagined before hand.

- The merger creates a church with two or more factions, who never bond fully. They may not be factions at war with each other, just people who don't mix well. And so the ministry limps along, leaders unaligned, probably declining in strength, steadily aging. Or, one group drifts away and leaves the other, almost a survival of the fittest scenario (or survival of the stubbornest). Don't be surprised in this scenario if the last people hanging on are older and meaner than the ones who left.

• When the merger is multi-site (meaning that we retained more than one church campus), great care must be taken to really merge things church-wide, or we end up with the same people basically in the same pews, but structurally joined one to another. You have to mix it up.

A merger could still lead to a great season of ministry. One of my three home churches that I mentioned earlier was a healthy merger back in 1928 – and it has continued to thrive in ministry now for almost a century since then, across multiple generations and cultural changes.

RECOMMENDED TOOL:

Vital Mergers by Dirk Elliott, 2013. In this book, Elliott explains the kind of mergers that almost always work well: marked by divesting of property and a new pastor skilled for the work of church planting – so that the merged church looks forward to a great start connected to its community, like a church plant.

A merger may be right for your church if:

- You have found another group of people with whom you believe you can build a ministry: people that are fun to be with and that energize you.

- The two churches each bring distinct gifts to the table. Sometimes the older church brings larger per capita giving to anchor the church in its early months. Perhaps the younger church brings technological savvy or relational connections to rising population groups in the area.

- Leaders from both (or all) churches are willing to spend some effort at creating a new church with a fresh vision that fully integrates the best of the antecedent churches. Leaders from the merging churches are willing to work together and bond as one team.

- Together, the new larger group is committed to let go of the past, the old buildings and the old church names. In this way, they demonstrate a commitment to act like a new church and start fresh in a new place, with a new identity, focused on a certain neighborhood or demographic in the community.[7]

- You can discipline yourselves not to claim victory when the merger produces a larger crowd or a

---

7   Often the merged church keeps one of the facilities but plans a major overhaul so that it essentially becomes a new place, designed for the people who have never yet walked in the doors.

fuller choir loft than either church has seen in years. A great first Sunday in a merged church is dangerous. It can distract from the evangelistic work that is yet required in the neighborhood.

- The new church has access to the kind of pastoral leader who can plant a new church. While this pastor might already be attached to one of the antecedent churches, she most likely will come along after the churches have merged, or at the time of merger. If they do not find the right pastoral leader, the merger will struggle.

This strategy might be challenging for your church if:

- The primary motivation for the merger (for either church) is survival of the church rather than blessing the neighborhood.

- The churches coming together are just too different in terms of theology or ethnic heritage to find a common ground for the creation of a common life. It is okay if this is the case – there are other strategies less difficult than merging.

- One of the buildings becomes the tail that wags the dog because of its amazing stained glass or its two million dollar pipe organ or its perfect acoustics. Once the building wags the church, it will be extremely hard to keep priorities straight as a new church is formed. Buildings will not fit through the eye of a needle – and they must never become non-negotiable for a church that is on a pilgrim journey.

5. **Marking the end of your church's ministry and bequeathing your facility and assets to another church or team with the know-how to grow ministry in your neighborhood.**

Some of you may still choose to stay around and enjoy the party. But you are tired of trying to run the party.

This strategy takes courage. A church must see the handwriting on the wall in terms of its future apart from an infusion of new leadership and energy. The church chooses to hand over the keys and the assets to another church – either the launch team of a brand new church emerging in the neighborhood or a mega-church that specializes in adopting struggling congregations and turning their buildings into campuses of the mega-church. In either case, the people who have run things let go. They stop running things, and release all assets to another group that they believe is more equipped to develop thriving ministry.

RECOMMENDED TOOLS:

Most denominations have tools available to guide a church that is contemplating and/or moving through formal closing. Two resources that have been helpful across denominational lines are L. Gail Irwin, *Toward the Better Country: Church Closure and Resurrection,* 2014 or Stephen Gray and Frank Dumond, *Legacy Churches*, 2009.

This strategy may be right for your church if:

- Your people are just getting tired of all the work entailed in keeping the doors open.

- You are finally running out of money to supplement the annual income short fall. Hopefully, you realize what time it is before the money runs out, so that your church's savings can be invested in the new ministry.

- The thought that another group might take the baton and keep working this ministry territory and worshiping in your building brings joy to your hearts. This makes it easier to say the benediction on your church's season of ministry.

- (Not required) You find a church that really carries forward your church's sense of call and DNA. This is more likely to be the case if the new church is of the same denomination as the declining church.

- Your building and savings accounts represent a positive asset that could help the next ministry to get planted well. (In some cases, the building is worth almost nothing on the market due to deferred maintenance issues, and so it cannot really help a new church.)

This strategy may be challenging for your church if:

- Selling the building energizes your leaders, as they imagine possibilities of the church's thriving beyond the albatross of endless maintenance, the oversized rooms and lack of accessibility. The church that has the vision to continue beyond its current building may again become a formidable ministry force.
- Your people are discovering a new sense of vision for the next chapter of ministry.

Marking the end of your church's ministry in this neighborhood, selling your assets to another church or entity, and going with a remnant of pioneer spirits to plant fresh in a new place.

This strategy got a bad rap in the mid twentieth century when so many White congregations fled racially changing neighborhoods, following their members from the cities into the suburbs. Honestly, some of those moves were not driven so much by racism as by pragmatics – the churches simply recognized that another team would be more effective in the neighborhood than they could ever be. I recall visiting First United Methodist Church Carrollton, Texas 20 years ago as a consultant, driving past community signage in Spanish and Korean as I approached their building. When I arrived I asked for a show of hands "How many of you can speak Korean?" No hands.

"How many of you can speak Spanish?" Two hands.

I recommended they sell to a church better equipped for that community. And that is what they did. They would likely have died in that location.

It isn't just White churches that may follow a diaspora of their members as they move to a new part of the community. A Black church in our downtown DC neighborhood followed its members into the Maryland suburbs early in this century as the DC Black population began to decline, replaced by young apartment and condo dwellers of multiple ethnic identities. The church had purchased their downtown building from a historic synagogue decades earlier, after the synagogues' constituency had migrated to Far Northwest DC and to Bethesda.

Now in a new century, as the Black church prepared to move, a group of Jewish developers bought their building. And they turned it back into a synagogue in response to the influx of Jewish young adults coming into the neighborhood. There is nothing necessarily wrong with this story.[8] People groups move around. Housing stock ages. Re-development happens. Immigrant communities pop up. Cities are dynamic. Most church buildings are located where their church members lived when the building was built.

Relocation may be right for your church if...

- A good portion of your church population is moving en masse to a new part of town. You could become a key church in that new part of town.

- It is unlikely that many in your church will develop the necessary cultural competencies to adapt to the new people moving in around your current church facility in order to partner and/or offer effective ministry.

- Rather than waste away in a situation where your church is going to steadily decline, your leaders

---

[8] This is not an endorsement of un-regulated urban gentrification, where affordable housing is lost and low-income populations are displaced. In the case of the church in this story, their church population was mostly middle class.

would rather relocate while you still have the resources to do so.

- Your church has the financial resources to build or purchase a new facility after selling your present facility (or the tenacity to thrive in borrowed space until you can raise and save the funds).

- Your current location has become more problematic. Perhaps the building has extremely poor visibility or difficult access, or the residential population around your church building has declined (due to loss of housing stock or expansion of a commercial corridor). Maybe it was built in the center of the population 75 years ago, and now it is far from the major traffic because the community grew a different direction.

Relocation may not work for your church if...

- Your building has special historical significance to your denomination or community, so that you feel some responsibility to care for it and to preserve it. You would not be able to sell it to just anyone.

- There is a cemetery in the adjacent land to the current building. In this case, you could decide to keep the current building as a multi-purpose space, which could be partly commercial (to create income that could be paid toward another space), and to simply worship elsewhere without investing heavily in a second property.

- The cost of equivalent space would be significantly more expensive elsewhere (in which case you could consider renting worship space and keeping the building for offices and midweek events).

- Your church's core constituency still lives all around the current building. If the building is a major problem, you could look at moving just a few blocks, if you can find a more workable space. This is what HopeGateWay Church in Portland, Maine did a decade ago.

Each of the above strategies requires different levels of cultural competency on the part of your church. Some will stretch you – others not so much. Each of the above strategies has proven to be a right answer for certain churches. And none of these strategies would be appropriate for every church.

It surprised me, writing this, how often in thinking about culturally competent ministry to our neighbors, the conversation still drifts back to the question of physical facility. It would be great to simply think about a church's gifts and calling apart from real estate. In the years ahead, we expect that many churches can downsize in terms of physical facility due to online participants and more varied worship times (with fewer persons at any given hour). However, real estate will continue to play a significant role in church development. A church has to meet somewhere – and for most of Christian history in virtually every nation on earth, churches have tended to own their houses of worship.

Hopefully as you continue this conversation with your sisters and brothers, you can be intentional in starting with your church's sense of mission, and then thinking the cultural implications, and only then assess questions of real estate.

PROCESSING THE STRATEGIES:

1. Did this review of pros and cons related to these six strategies offer you any new insights or thoughts?

2. Is there a strategy that might fit your church that has not been discussed much? Would you like to put it on the table?

3. How might the strategy that has caught your imagination require renewed cultural competency for your church?

4. Who would you like to invite into the conversation as your process the strategies of interest?

Cultural Competency Began as a Work of the Holy Spirit, and So It Continues

Every church can do work to get more prepared for the ministry God calls it to. We sometimes have to learn new languages, requiring hours of study. We have to get out into community, requiring hours of listening and partnering. We have to examine our social and racial privilege in terms of how it blinds us to ourselves and sabotages any Good News that we seek to advance in the world. But finally, cultural competency is a Gift of the Spirit. We do our homework, but that homework is never enough. Human homework did not power the Book of Acts.

Finally, we depend on the Holy Spirit to take the Good News across cultural boundaries, some of which we have built with our own hypocrisy. I invite your Expedition Team to do the hard work it needs to do – and then to call upon the Spirit to empower you and lead you forward on the Greatest Expedition of your lives.

the greatest
EXPEDITION

greatestexpedition.com

REACH NEW PEOPLE

The Greatest Expedition

GREATESTEXPEDITION.COM

Nineteen leaders you know and trust have been working more than a year to create 20 books, leadership materials, expedition maps, and events for local congregations, districts, conferences and other groups.

SUE NILSON KIBBEY
Breakthrough Prayer

PHIL MAYNARD
Venture Preparation

KAY KOTAN
Assessing the Current Venture

PAUL NIXON
Cultural Competency

OLU BROWN
A New Kind of Clergy Venture Leader

KELLY BROWN
Equipping Lay Venture Leaders

JAYE JOHNSON
Expedition Accountability

KEN WILLARD
The What, Why and Where of The New Expedition

KENDA CREASY-DEAN
Expanding the Expedition Through Social Innovation

DAN JACKSON
Generative Leadership

BLAKE BRADFORD
Strengthening Decision-Making and Governance

CHRISTIAN COON
Evangelizing the Christian

JASON MACKEY
Intentional New Relational Building

MILES WELCH
Creating and Sustaining a Prevailing Expedition

DAN PEREZ
Community Connection

RACHEL GILMORE
Missional Communities

KEN NASH
Expanding the Expedition through Multi-Sites

WAYNE SCHMIDT
Marketplace Multipliers

NICOLE REILLY
Expanding the Expedition through Digital Ministry

To explore how to set your church out on a new adventure to become more relevant and contextual to reach new people in your community, visit:

greatestexpedition.com

Market Square BOOKS

Made in United States
North Haven, CT
09 February 2022

15887248R00055